MW01100943

To The Parents:

Our farm has many animals living together. We believe all these animals have the right to live a full and happy life with lots of love and attention.

Most farm animal books talk about how the animal can help people but this book is intended to share fun facts and photos about the animals and enrich the understanding and appreciation of the them and their unique personalities.

Farming practices are often called into question – our farm is a family farm with the intent to turn it into a rescue center. We see too many animals being hurt and poorly treated or abandoned.

We are not condoning any specific lifestyle but encourage people to treat animals with respect and gain a better understanding of how animals and people can co-exist.

Text and illustrations (digitally enhanced original photos) by Selene Muldowney
Design courtesy I.J. James
Visit us at www.pinkmartinidesigns.com

ISBN: 978-0-9913974-1-9

Welcome to the Farmstead!

There are many animals on a farm – sometimes they stay a long time and sometimes they only visit for a little while. Farm animals, like all animals, are special and often have different personalities. They, like all living creatures, want food, water, love, and shelter. Animals do not communicate with words but make their own unique sounds and vocalize when they are happy, sad, angry, and frightened.

On our farm we make sure all the animals are given proper nutrition and care. Our sheep grow wool in the winter and during the summer months they get very hot so we sheer them. The llamas also grow long fibers, and not only get hot in the summer months, but also get all sorts of bramble, sticks, and dirt stuck in them. We have to take special care of our animals. They rely on us, and since they don't speak our language, we have to learn how to communicate with them.

Our momma ducks live on the pond, and when they have babies, they will often introduce them to us. We take the mommas and babies and keep them safe in a pen away from predators like wild coyotes and other animals while they are still young and growing. When the baby ducks have their feathers and can fly away we let them all out on the pond; they live together with the other ducks.

Our dogs love the farm and help all the other animals stay safe. The cats also love the farm, and do their share by cuddling with the baby sheep we sometimes have to bring into the house.

Baby animals are fun and cute, but need lots of work and care. They should stay with their momma as long as they can although sometimes they need a little extra help so we have to feed them with bottles and keep warm lights on them. Once they have learned to nurse from their momma and are stronger they are allowed to join the rest of their family.

Our animals have learned to co-exist on the farm. They share their unique personalities with us. Our hope is to share what it is like to live on a farm with so many different animals who have become part of our family. Like other families, we have to take care of each family member and make sure they have a happy home. Our animals share a special place in our hearts, and as we have learned to co-exist with them, we hope you will appreciate how special each animal is and remember they rely on each of us to be good stewards of the earth. From feathers to paws we know each animal, each pet, each creature that walks this earth deserves a full and happy life – our goal is to create a happy and healthy environment with them.

Meet
HIGHTOP
the Llama

hmmmm

LLAMA
l.glama

* A male llama is a sire, the female a dam, and cria is the name given to baby llama.

* A group of llamas is called herd.

* Llamas have two-toed feet

* Llamas are compared to dogs and horses because of their trustworthiness and capability to carry heavy loads.

* Llamas are intelligent animals and can be easily trained.

* They are peaceful and calm animals; however, will spit when agitated.

* Llamas are covered in fireproof wool.

About Hightop & Bisquit:

These two fellows love carrots and broccoli and will come over to the fence and ask for snacks. They are very friendly and like to visit with us. They are smart and often we refer to them as our llama puppies.

Meet
BISQUIT
the Llama

PIGS

SUS

* Pigs are intelligent animals. They are the fourth smartest animal on the planet.

* They are omnivores, meaning they eat both plants and other animals.

* They can life on average up to the age of 15.

* Pigs are very clean animals. They do not like to use the bathroom where they sleep or eat.

* A male pig is called a boar, a female pig is a sow, a baby pig is called a piglet.

* Pigs have small lungs.

* Pigs drink up to 14 gallons of water every day.

* Pigs are easily trained to walk on a leash, use a litter box and do tricks.

About Queenie & Hoggers:

Our precious pigs love company and will spend hours playing, sunbathing, and chatting. Queenie loves her snout rubbed and will ask for her ears and back to be scratched.

Meet **QUEENIE** the Pig

OINK
OINK
OINK
OINK

Meet
BIG MOMMA
the Cow

MOOOOOOooooooo.......

Cows
Bos taurus

* Cattle are herbivores that eat vegetation such as grass.

* Adult females are called cows, young cattle are calves, adult males are called bulls.

* There are more than 800 different breeds of cattle around the world.

* Cows (cattle) form close friendships and choose to spend much of their time with 2-4 preferred individuals. They also hold grudges for years and may dislike particular individuals.

* They have an excellent sense of smell. They can detect odors up to five miles away. They can also hear both low and high frequency sounds beyond human capability.

About Big Momma, Mocha, & Latte:

Momma cow is very protective of her babies and while she lets us rub their ears and feed them snacks she is always nearby. They all love plums and apple slices

Meet
BIG RED
& VALENTINO
the Ram & Lamb

BAAAAAA!

SHEEP
Ovis aries

* Sheep are herbivores that eat vegetation such as grass.

* Female sheep are called ewes, male sheep are called rams, and baby sheep are called lambs.

* A group of sheep is known as a herd, flock or mob.

* Sheep have good memories and can remember at least 50 individual sheep and humans for years. They do this by using a similar neural process and part of the brain that humans use to remember.

* They are extremely intelligent animals capable of problem solving. They are considered to have a similar IQ level to cattle and are nearly as clever as pigs.

About Big Red & Valentino:

Our adorable father and son found a moment to cuddle while getting their feet cleaned. Valentino was born early and stopped breathing. We gave him CPR and took special care of him until he was strong enough to stay with his family.

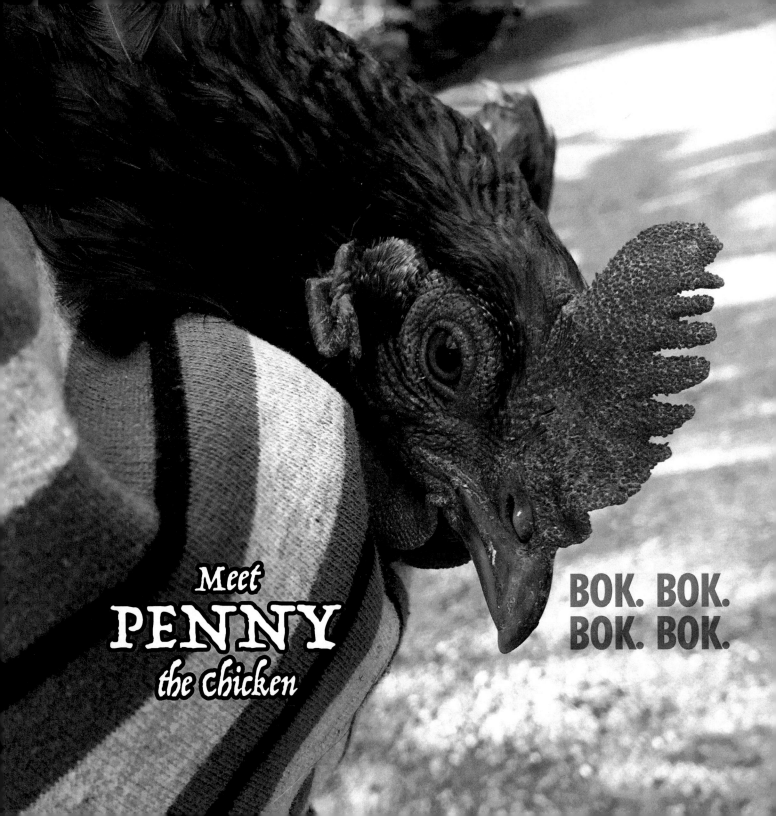

Meet
PENNY
the chicken

BOK. BOK.
BOK. BOK.

CHICKENS
Gallus gallus domesticus

* Male chickens are called roosters, cocks or cockerels, depending on the country, Female chickens are pullets until they're old enough to lay eggs and become hens.

* Baby chickens are chicks.

* They are omnivores and will eat seeds, insects, small mice, and lizards.

* Chickens form complex social orders often called "Pecking Order"

* Chickens have over 30 types of vocalizations and even talk to their young before they are hatched.

About Penny, Helga, Blondie:

We have three chickens who follow us everywhere and often will snuggle and cuddle with us while we are outside.
Penny likes to tell the other chickens what to do. Blondie and Helga always help us harvest the garden. Penny likes grapes and will eat them before we can pick them.

BARN SWALLOW
Hirundo rustica

* The Barn swallow is a migratory bird that belongs to the group of songbirds.

* They fly in a zigzag manner at the speed of approximately 36 feet per second.

* They often fly close to the surface of the ground and water and feed during the flight.

* Barn swallows often build nests under man-made structures such as barns, stables, buildings and bridges.

* Nests are semi-circular in shape and are made out of the mud, bird's saliva and leaves.

* Barn swallows eat different types of large insects including flies, beetles, wasps, butterflies, moths and bees.

About our Barn Swallows:

These babies are always asking for food. They are newborn and very hungry so their parents take turns looking for food and protecting them. We have several families living in our barn. They let us know if we are too close to their nests but don't mind when we leave them food.

woof

Meet
DAESHA,
LULU BELL,
COWBOY, &
HARLEY D
the Dogs

woof

woof

woof

DOGS
Canis lupus familiaris

* Dogs are the domesticated descendents of wolves. Their shared ancestry has been traced back 37 to 58 million years, to a five-toed, weasel-like animal called Miacis. There are nearly 500 recognized breeds of domestic dog.

* Dog nose prints are as unique as a human finger prints and can be used to accurately identify them.

* Dogs' sense of hearing is ten times more acute than a humans.

* A Dog's whiskers -- found on the muzzle, above the eyes and below the jaws -- are technically known as vibrissae. They are touch-sensitive hairs than actually sense minute changes in airflow.

About Daesha, Cowboy, Lulu Belle, & Harley D:

Loyal, friendly, and always there to comfort us - these pups are part of our family. Each of them has a distinct personalty. Cowboy forgets what he is doing and sometimes needs a reminder, Deasha loves food and tennis balls, Harley D likes wearing clothes and loves belly rubs, and Lulu Belle can walk for hours and hours and hours.

CATS
Felis catus

* On average, cats spend 2/3 of every day sleeping.

* While it is commonly thought that the ancient Egyptians were the first to domesticate cats, the oldest known pet cat was recently found in a 9,500-year-old grave on the Mediterranean island of Cyprus.

* Cats make about 100 different sounds.

* They can jump up to five times its own height in a single bound.

* A cat's heart beats nearly twice as fast as a human heart.

* Cats purr when they appear to be content, but also purr when they're giving birth, sick, nursing, wounded, or in a stressful situation.

About Tiger Wayne & Tinker Bell:

These cats and their visiting friends believe they are in charge of the farm and want to be treated as royalty. They spend every minute of every day around us. They often can be found supervising us while we work on the farm.

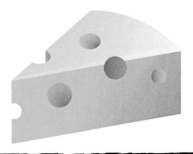

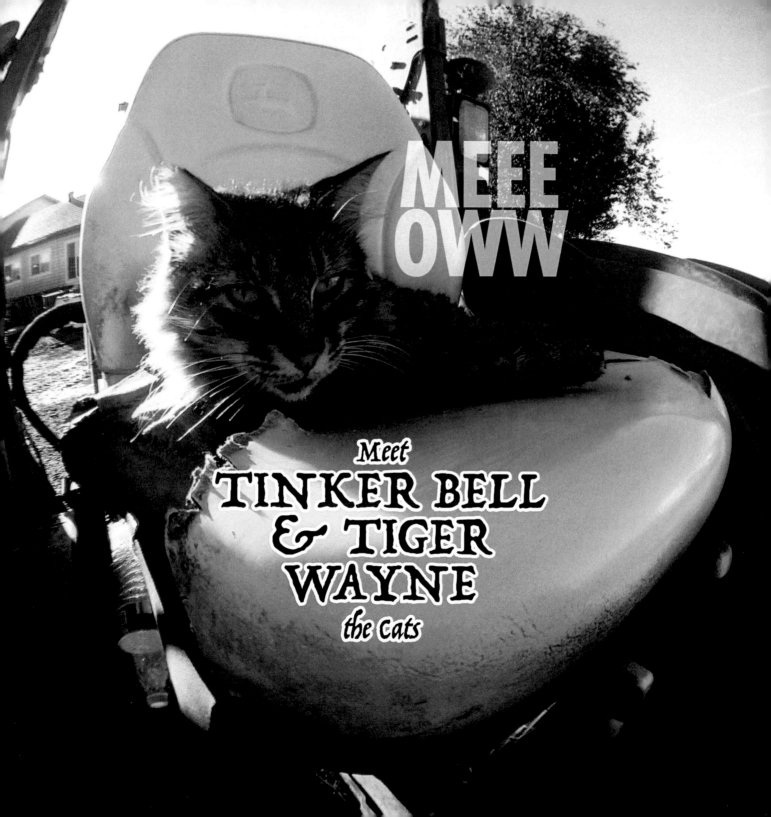

MEEE OWW

Meet
**TINKER BELL
& TIGER
WAYNE**
the cats

GEESE
Anser anser domesticus & Anser cygnoides

* A goose is often characterized by a long neck, web footed, non-iridescent coloration and its honk.

* They are typically gregarious migratory aquatic birds

* The female goose lays 1 egg each day, until a full clutch of about five eggs is obtained.

* A female is commonly called a goose, a male a gander, and a young bird is called a gosling.

* The goose mainly eats grains, snails, frogs, and small animals.

* They honk as a form of communication.

* A group of geese is called a gaggle.

About The Collective:

These geese have an important job and they do it well - they keep a watchful eye on the other birds and protect them from predators. They love attention and often ask us to turn on the sprinkler.

quack
QUACK

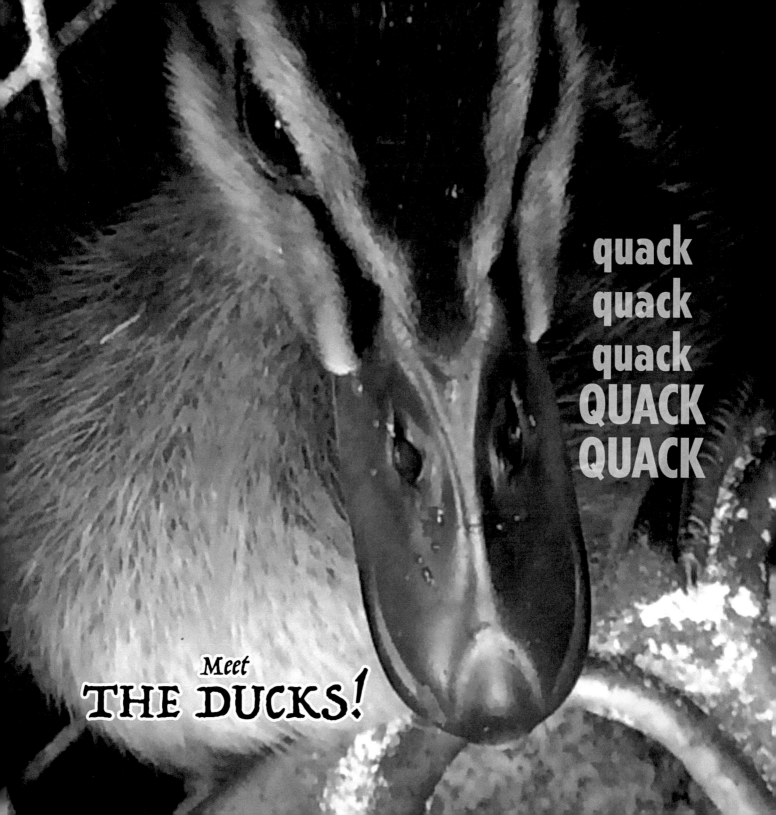

quack
quack
quack
QUACK
QUACK

Meet
THE DUCKS!

DUCKS
Anas platyrhynchos

* An adult male duck is a drake, adult female is called a hen or a duck, a baby is called a duckling, and a group of ducks can be called a raft, team or paddling.

* All ducks have highly waterproof feathers.

* They have three eyelids.

* Duck feet have no nerves or blood vessels so they do not feel the cold! This allows ducks to swim in icy water, and walk in ice and snow.

* Ducks are related to geese and swans but have shorter necks and wings and a stout body.

About The Ducks:

Domestic or wild, we welcome all the ducks to the farm. They always greet us at the door asking for breakfast, lunch, dinner, and snacks. They will respond when called - they also talk back! Farm life isn't the same without ducks.

Meet HEFTY the horse

neigh

HORSE
Equus ferus caballus

* A male horse is called a stallion, female is called a mare, a young male is called a colt and young female is called a filly.

* Horses are herbivores (plant eaters).

* Horses like sweet flavors and will usually reject anything sour or bitter.

* Horses drink at least 25 gallons of water a day (more in hotter climates).

* They have been found in cave paintings that date back to around 15000 B.C.

* Horses can sleep both lying down and standing up.

* Horses have bigger eyes than any other mammal that lives on land.

* Horses have better memories than an elephant

About Hefty:

Hefty is a sweet boy with a naughty personality. He can unlock gates and sneak out. He likes to take the apples out of the basket and won't let the other animals eat until he gets his first bite.

GOAT
Capra aegagrus hircus

* Male goats are bucks, females are called does, and baby goats are called kids.

* Goats communicate with each other by bleating.

* Mother goats will often call to their young (kids) to ensure they stay close-by.

* Goats have rectangular eyes - which allows them to see very well in the dark.

* They are social animals although they are not flock-orientated.

* Goats live eight to twelve years.

* Goats are good swimmers.

About our goats:

Goats are very mischievous and constantly will knock over barrels and buckets. They love to climb and play. They are very protective but once they get to know you are friendly.

MAAAA

Meet
THE GOATS

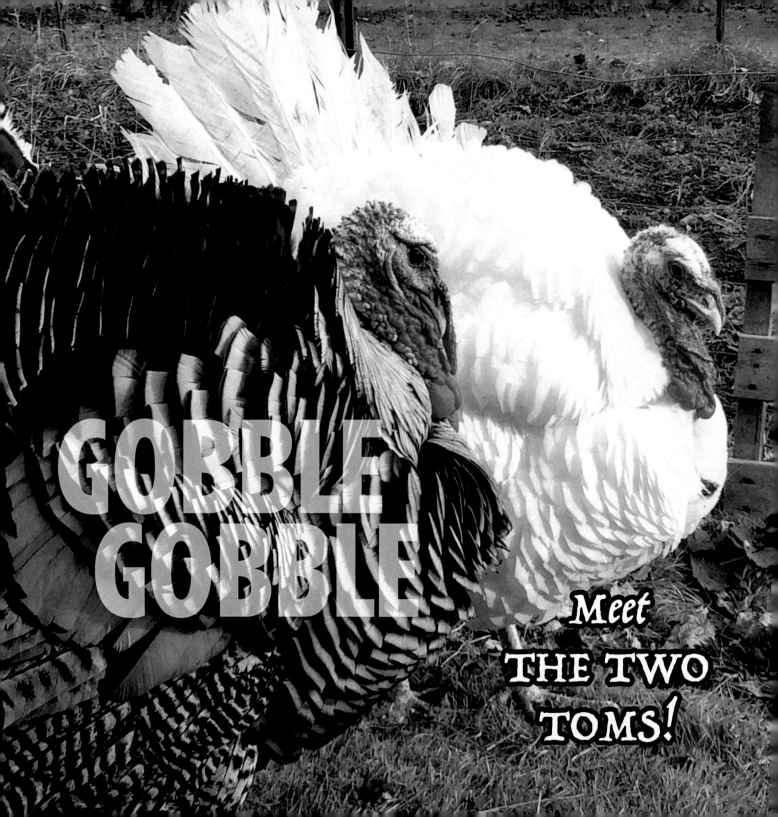

GOBBLE
GOBBLE

Meet
THE TWO
TOMS!

TURKEY
Meleagris

* Male turkeys are called "gobblers," after the "gobble" call they make to announce themselves to females.

* Females are called hens.

* A turkey's gender can be determined from its droppings:
  Males produce spiral-shaped poop and
  Females poop is shaped like the letter J.

* The color of a turkey's head and throat change depending on their mood.

* They form strong social bonds with their families and flock mates.

* Turkeys have great hearing despite no external ears,

* They have an amazing field of vision and can see in color.

* The turkey has a gizzard as part of its stomach containing tiny stones to aid in digestion.

About Two Toms:

These two boys grew up together, and while sometimes they argue, they get upset if they are separated. They spend all day together and will follow us, the chickens, and geese around the garden. They love snacks and attention.

Let's be FRIENDS

besties

 www.joaquinthedog.org

 @Joaquin_Around_The_World

READ MORE »

Joaquin Around San Diego
Joaquin Around Boston
Joaquin Around Los Angeles
Joaquin Around San Francisco
Joaquin Around Washington DC
Joaquin Around New Orleans
Joaquin Around Denver
Joaquin Around Cape Cod
Joaquin Around the Holidays
Joaquin Around the Office

Coming Soon!!
Joaquin Around Mexico City
and more!

ABOUT THE AUTHOR

Selene Muldowney lives with her family on a farm on Whidbey Island, a quiet island just north of Seattle, surrounded by an amazing assortment of animals that have all adopted her. A writer and marketing consultant, she can often be found knee-deep in mud - surrounded

by hooves, feathers, paws, fur, and fiber. Known to paddle into a pond to save some baby ducks or other wildlife, Muldowney is an advocate for all people and animals, with an endless energy to help others. A loving mom, an advocate for animals, and someone with a creative conscience, Muldowney brings out the best in those around her. She finds beauty in the smallest of things, and is known to be distracted by everything around her. She is also a world traveler, born in Africa, fluent in Spanish and still learning French, Italian, and Japanese.

DEDICATION:

This book is dedicated to all the animals who have shared our farmstead with us over the years. Some of our companions have died, and while we miss them, we know their memory remains in our hearts; they have made our lives so much richer and fuller. We miss you Hightop, Hefty, and Lulu Belle. Thank you for teaching us to be better stewards of the earth and to love without limits.

TESTIMONIAL:

Increasingly, more enlightened thinking is fuelling a movement to reduce the suffering endured by millions of farm animals worldwide. In her children's book, "Paws, Wings, Hooves & Hope On The Farmstead", author Selene Muldowney through words and images hopes to influence young minds by introducing them to the unique personalities of farm animals that reside on her family farm. With names like "Hightop the Llama" and sheep with names such as "Big Red & Valentino," children are sure to be delighted and will likely request repeated readings before bedtime.

Jett Britnell
Writer & Photographer

Made in the USA
San Bernardino, CA
18 September 2015